# MODERN CURRICULUM PRESS
Cleveland • Toronto

# How Can I, Dainty Dinosaur?

by

**Babs Bell Hajdusiewicz**

**illustrated by Diana Noro**

**Modern Curriculum Press, Inc.**
A Division of Simon & Schuster
13900 Prospect Road
Cleveland, OH 44136

**Library of Congress Cataloging-in-Publication Data**

Hajdusiewicz, Babs Bell, 1944–
  How can I, Dainty Dinosaur?

  Summary: A little girl's imaginary dinosaur helps her to
make a decision about taking her favorite blanket to a
slumber party.
  [1. Blankets—Fiction. 2. Fear—Fiction. 3. Imaginary
playmates—Fiction. 4. Dinosaurs—Fiction] I. Title.
PZ7.H128175Ho 1988        [E]        87–24804

ISBN 0-8136-5226-X (hardcover)
ISBN 0-8136-5726-1 (paperback)

123456789     92 91 90 89 88

I do want to go!
May I?
May I sleep there, too?

Oh, Dainty Dinosaur.
It will be fun.
I will play and play.
I will sleep there, too.

Dainty Dinosaur!
Dainty Dinosaur!
What is it?
Come here, Dainty Dinosaur.

7

Oh!
That is it!
You do not want
me to go.

But you will
come, too.

Yes, yes.
You will come.
This will come, too.
Go to sleep now, Dainty Dinosaur.

Get up.
Get up, Dainty Dinosaur.
This is the day.

We will go there.
You and I and this will go.
What fun it will be!

Come, Dainty Dinosaur.
We have things to do.

We will need this.
It will help us.
We will take
things in it.

13

I will need this.
And this.
And this.
And this, too.

Oh, no, Dainty Dinosaur!
How can I go?
What will I do?

16

I have to take this.
But how can I?
No, I can not go.

They will see it.
They will make fun of it.
They will make fun of me.
I have to take it, but how can I take it?

But I want to go.
Can I put it here?
Will this work?

No, they will see it.
They will laugh.
Oh, oh, oh.
How can I go and take it?

Oh, Dainty Dinosaur!
Look at you.
That is how!
You are a help to me.

I will put it in here.
Yes, this will do it.
They will not see it.
But it will be there for me to sleep.

WCA

This is it, Dainty Dinosaur.
We will go in.
We will play here.
We will sleep here, too.

22

I like this.
Look, look.
Do you like it?

LOBBY

23

What will we do?
This?
This?

We can do this now.
Look, Dainty Dinosaur.
This is fun.

That was fun.
We will go to sleep now.

Oh, oh, Dainty Dinosaur.
What if they do see it?
What will I do?

27

Look, look, look!
There is one.
And one there.
And one there, too.

This is good.
They will see.
But no one will laugh.

This is fun.
You are here with me.
I am here with you.
It is here with us.
We can go to sleep now.

31

Babs Bell Hajdusiewicz, author and poet, is the originator of Pee Wee Poetry™. She is a former teacher and school administrator and lives in Rocky River, Ohio.

*How Can I, Dainty Dinosaur?* uses the 64 words listed below.

| | | |
|---|---|---|
| a | I | see |
| am | if | sleep |
| and | in | |
| are | is | take |
| at | it | that |
| | | the |
| be | laugh | there |
| but | like | they |
| | look | thing (s) |
| can | | this |
| come | make | to |
| | may | too |
| dainty | me | |
| day | | up |
| dinosaur | need | us |
| do | no | |
| | not | want |
| for | now | was |
| fun | | we |
| | of | what |
| get | oh | will |
| go | one | with |
| good | | work |
| | play | |
| have | put | yes |
| help | | you |
| here | | |
| how | | |

Ej          Hajdusiewicz, Babs Bell
                How can I, Dainty Dinosaur?

                            41729

AP21 '89
NO21 '89